Be the thing of memory

Carrie Olivia Adams

Tolsun Books
Flagstaff, Arizona

Be the thing of memory

Edited by Heather Lang-Cassera.

Cover photo by Heather Lang-Cassera.
Artwork in cover photo by Dante Gabriel Rossetti.
Cover design by Brandi Pischke and David Pischke.

Set in Adobe Garamond Pro 12 pt font.
Design by David Pischke.

ISBN 978-1-948800-41-9

Published by Tolsun Publishing, Inc., Flagstaff, Arizona.
www.tolsunbooks.com

for STA (eternity & always)

Contents

Be the thing of memory

Daughter of a Tree Farm

Drawn from erasures of the *Autobiography of Countess Tolstoy* (1922)

For a long time, I did not know better. For a long time, I did not know anything else. The daughter of a tree farm, I could not see the road. When someone said: you are what I need, I let the weight be the mass of me. I'd leave the trees and my arms would be full of scrapes that I never felt happening. I moved deeper into their very straight lines, into the branches. Their order brushed against my shoulders as I ran. And it was all sap and itch; I was marked. And when you said: *you*. Well, what did I know? I listened. And the thing about the farm is that it's quiet.

Slate stones and horizons that curve. The circumstances under which, and through which, we grow. Readers may consider that which bleeds and heals, elaborate. But the question of *going away* roused the most passionate interest. Due, no doubt, to the disciples and opponents watching the will [and the windy gestures] of the going away from the hillside. All of us, a few short appendices, points, and persons.

My age is not in doubt. I had not yet ruined all I had to ruin to convince myself. In the wood rings, there is an age of belief. I could run into the pines and meet a stranger there. The most free thing was still a full moon and a sky-lit gravel road. Halter and bit, I was yet bound by a strategic reticence.

I shall hardly cut my family. It is unknown whether I fulfilled my promise. The most difficult thing is the will to fix the moment from devotion. I am continually wondering whether I am doing it properly. And whether tomorrow, pardon.

The pity smell of fresh cut wood, followed by the taste of a deer's block. I should say that the tree farm failed. Or lost interest. Today, it must be a football field of forest surrounded by hay. Within, its own ecosystem of creatures. One summer it must have seemed like a thing to do. To focus on the building of a grid with string. To mark each square with little colored flags and then a little tree, one by one by one. What else was there to do?

Be so good as you. To which I reply: you want more facts. There is a bit of *Alice* in everything. If I had a daughter, I would tell her to always know what kind of story she's in. But I lived in my. And loved it when it was dark. I only vaguely realized I was in the winter of my investigations with regard, new instructions required. Me, at the fortune, belonging by fire. Remember when we'd set the woods on fire?

My father and mother, a daughter. The branches that obscured the view. The same fortuned while embroidering a private govern language. The itch of a secret. The distance lent me the simplicity of reduction. Everything in correlations of atoms, but want of the ordinary. I gave up forever at home. In life I remember present, read to represent a promise concentrating, carried away. A great many books ending with *I was fascinated and surprised*. That tongue developed out of the feeble growth of a living creature.

In the dark of the farm, we would sit till late. At that time I tried very hard. It was in a letter wrote little and rarely replied. With us, every new idea or the carrying of some instance wrote upon me the idea of history. My father, it was because he felt the beauty of his own creations that time was not bad. I realize serving has given strength. I also make war. And peace, when I am carried away. Sometimes, all the winter had *be*en read to me.

When a material, namely miserable, muffled-up. In November, I sent it to my harm. I was often astonished and could not understand why, corrected or destroyed, I used to be delighted. Sometimes, a request or a gram would be sent to substitute. My whole became instance, frequent repetitions of the same wooden point. Sometimes, my remarks explain my clumsy afterwards.

Some passages in war, the hunting party in peace, aloud from a distance—these are allowed often in life, when works not only move but grieve suddenly. Haven't I remembered the old oak forest near the house lighted up by the sun and the fields? Dictated to me. Passed away home.

Belonging by fire. A beehive's swarm of bees attacking a bear, made small. Finishing to earn the honor of departure. Remarkable, against my will, to liaison the leaves.

It was so windy there. Our family had not seen our way back. How to combat the farm's idleness? The itch of still. I did not think it was possible. I shall go and tell everything or shoot. The force of the need. Fate and activity began to consider their origin but did not like to be called in. I remember now how to listen to anything new. We lived a recall that passed us by; we followed nothing. I desired nothing else but to develop as though they were living. I had no other proof.

During the first years, I tried to follow it as well as I could. The miniscule unfurling of growth. Very often between and sometimes flattering. The early summer, whole days among the hives. And the hay. Everywhere in the grass, glow worms began to shine. In my hand and on the earth. Perhaps undeserved, I thank intention. Portraits for some reason were never like me. Now little.

When children can no longer devote sympathy, owing to their growing up. One mind always engaged or found with labor in order to be. Later on the trees acquired winter. Sent and took and did not go out. The weight of never shedding. We anticipated a cure if it comes willingly. We were unable to carry out nature. These impressions, fresh, often made me see his life previous, the principal sadness I had to recognize.

We planted trees. We cleared the pond. Gathered different, undisturbed faith. Gradually the steps further and further withdrawing over the hills, beyond the fencerow. I was too weak. I was often driven, but saw no way. I would never go back.

The difference, between us, not because I remained the same, unable to unalter, but taken from the midst, rarely clouded, and the broken. It was this, which woke me open, opened to an outsider, a stranger.

Young, I caught the point of death. Whether discontent and seeking, when he did not find. Without saying threatened to take, threatened to go away from despair—or believe. Our family, shuddered, could not find reconcile with the mind at rest. A spirit becoming turned through all that was beautiful, disappeared. To live ever changing direction.

I used to feel dull and wrote to him. Somehow or other it made me sad. That beautiful epic in book form, still growing. The way I looked back and could never quite touch it. Afterwards, the place would remain permanent, apart from this purpose. His great work: everyday life, setting fire to the fields. That smoke in both our hair.

We fell asleep while arriving. How to master families, tear away from the living in order to describe people. I still stop talking for long times. In me, our house, the farm, everywhere made so much of that which I sympathized. Everything true and pointed, up to the end.

Of my going away. With him it was a church turned in prayer. Remember the foundation. I did not understand why it had been created, grown by ourselves. If I had given away all my desire (I don't know to whom), I could have done nothing else. Alone, bore peace. In my turn, as I grew, I remember how I became especially helped. To live and to think, I often went for advice to reading books.

He used to entrust me to the work of making up sentences and of retelling sparrows and others. On appearance, which I never liked, I wrote a story from the woman's point of view. Later on, I wrote a tale, as if we were mad. I wanted to convey towards nature, grammar. I used to invent stories. I tried to imitate them. And who knows better where they now lie, waiting the verdict?

Whole days he mowed, discontent with the family. Secretly confessed to me about the horses, the ducks, the sounds that slowly trailed off and disappeared in mud, in the names of the forest we had grown. When going away forever, I could never forget that no one knew of it, handed over to me. This plea. A power to learn so intimate and common. I did not wish to own it, and I tried to get the gravel out of my ears. Nearest, take nothing. Myself, received and removed, mistaken in that world. I got to know this too late.

Distressed by the ardent sympathy of imagined. To part small, suffering satisfied the dream in the way of his carrying. There was always something in our arms. Yet, on the other hand, the method of life, sinking extraordinarily. We had walked in a slim figure of storm, of rain. It rolled with the hills as it arrived. Before, that summer in the evenings, I forgot for a time. To think of the infinite do not say anything definite, but rejoice vaguely.

I was always watching the farm from the window. And the driveway that curved past it out of view. I should go near, but not come in. After it became empty, the daughter lent pain. I remember for a while I used to sit at night. I used to go back again to our minds in the country, occupied with work. I worked hard at connection. I did not anticipate a memory, though. Moreover, by accident, I was completely carried away. I did not regret my final attempts of the woods.

We had to endure leaving to fight a low war or some other kind of murder. A peculiar pain in my heart when I saw others look in operation. How quietly I had prepared. I fell asleep. How insignificant. I seemed to be asking: what then is important.

To help one another to live. I think the same now.

The will wavered and then removed its hand. I recovered a heavy weight on our rift. Eventually with difficulty, in our keeping, we ceased.

On the stump of a tree, the will he wrote: I clearly see my mistake, my intention. *I ought to.* It is good to feel I cannot struggle clouded, deliberately, subtly upon the mind of an old man.

No longer concealed silence in front of us. To put an end, throwing into the pond some girl he could not get to return.

I felt no hunger. Later, the door was locked, and when I wanted to get a glimpse through the window, a curtain was drawn across it.

No one ever told him every one was afraid. Lying motionless I whispered the result of a terrible effort, come as an answer.

Look upon them as a trial of needles. *be done.*

The Pain Reliever

Based upon the writings of Sarah Hackett Stevenson and Alice Magaw, "The Mother of Anesthesia," and days spent amid the collections of the International Museum of Surgical Science

When I go under
I see the same things.
My hair always blowing.
There is always wind
or speed or the inability
to tell the difference
that is letting go of pain.

Anesthesia is like therapy,
only the doctor does all the talking.

There is no hurry.

It takes pain to remove pain
to know how to talk me to sleep.
I take my cue from the synesthesia blue,
a summer dark sky that smells like intentions.
My mistake was thinking I could be anything
other than hungry.

My mistake was thinking I could be anything other.
I too am the unmaking—
eyes that give the first signs of danger.

It takes pain to identify pain.
Snow might be required,
best carried in a wooden box
packed lightly with cotton wool.
In an ordinary huckaback hand towel
folded into three—
early methods of collecting
antecedents of the already misplaced.

Suggestion is a comfortable narcosis,
but never bid a patient breathe deep.
It takes pain to inspire confidence.
You must watch me get near the edge.

There is plenty of time.

It's the pulse that misleads
when I've fallen far.
It's been our mistake to confuse
sorrow for suffering—
which one do you see?

It began as a party game
so we could bump into things and never feel;
now it's the only way to get inside of me.

There is no hurry.

When the heart is acting badly
it's pleasant and easy to give.
With a few words of encouragement
I may let go of the wheel.

There is plenty of time.

I let you undo
quick—
far away train whistle,
ashes of a furnace furnished.
Those limbs beginning to bud again—
the plum tree scabs where the growth shoots.

We won't say saw
we'll elide the sound of breaking.

There is no hurry.

The branches bend to snap—
I ask grief pardon.
A bridge threatened to draw up;
choke pears too low, a vow, safe.
Do you know when to stop stitching?

The great secret of giving an anaesthetic
is not to feel hurried
to say occasionally *lots of time.*

Q. What are the contents of the cranium?

A. A small frozen lake, rusted cars, and forgotten mittens.

Q. What do you call the union of bones in the cranium?

A. Suture.

Q. What are the two kinds of sutures?

A. True and false.

Q. Do they communicate?

A. No, there is a plate between them.

Put your hands where the heart should be—
the breath becomes blood
the blood breath—
they are beat.

Percuss the chest:
what echo returns to you?

The answer is ready.
You will have vibrations
giving rise to sounds
as when we strike a wall with a hammer.

Can you wrap a wound that has no entry?

The butcher in you,
you made them wait,
you made it not-not messy.

Obscure the word rather than show it
show by obscuring
obscure by showing—

there are so many ways I could say body
without making you blush.

Of water, of work

a chest of drawers
an ambush of widows
a bank of circuits
a drift of bees

this bed of clams
bed of flowers
bed of oysters
bed of snakes—

a chisel, to free the bone completely.

In the treatment of fractures:
the assistant who holds the arm
should have nothing else to do.

There is a language of repair—
a muster of mendings
a prickle of prudence.

And these tiny bones
sawed away and the marrow exposed,
a small piece removed,
the cavity is made visible.

An atlas of ambush / assembly
an atlas of hands.

The islands of the brain
often communicate
though seldom unite.
The joint cleft
abducts the thumb.

The hand is an organ
not of touch alone—
I may even think with my fingers.

The important thing
is that the word knife
need never be mentioned.

The one with limb sorn
the one with the burn to be salved—
skin peels, skin tears away, skin melts—
it's so familiar like that:

how to reset
how to brace.

Wrapping the surface of the body
a thousand silvery nerve-strings
carry the message *a stranger waits outside.*

Q. On what bone do we lean when on our elbow?

A. The windowsill. The desk.

Q. What is the process called by which we lean?

A. The asking too much.

Q. When I am weary, I?

A. Allow an attachment for muscles and afford a bed for the ramification of vessels. (Ramification: a banded structure, act or process of branching)

Q. Describe the origin and insertion.

A. Will you show me the object?

Q. What is the situation in women?

A. It is not known.

Silence is the sound the knife makes
slitting the skin.

Can you identify my weakness,
a pricking sensation
and numbness in one limb?

Can you hold this tongue?
Tell me, what is the function
of meticulous courage.

You are the most yourself
when you are in the motion.

One can be quick and too quick.
I have a stomach too.
It gets hungry.

If I be of necessity
opportunity,
if there be the slightest chance of success,
why have a mind, if?

Does that scream in the night across the alley
beg an answer? Are we crowning
into the sludge of an injury and its repair?

An elephant is larger and stronger than a horse;
but it is not preferred as a beast of burden.

Strength is a wee umbrella
in the storm.

This the friction sound heard
in inspiration, expiration, or both.

For convenience of description,
blood is bright red and frothy.

Have you earned the privilege
of making mistakes?

There really is no sex in science.

The nomenclature lifts
delicate subjects up from the plane
in which language places them.

Man has more strength,
woman, more endurance.

The hands and the instruments
are the chief sources of danger.

This fever.

There is no subject on which so much has been written
and so little known.

Q. How is the tongue divided?

A. The tongue is divided into a basis and apex, a superior and inferior surface, and two edges.

A2. Those edges may be hard or soft.

Q. What is the heart?

A. The heart is a hollow, muscular viscus situated in the pericardium in the cavity of the thorax, resting upon the diaphragm.

Q. What are the depressions of the liver?

A. 1. The great fissure
2. A fissure for fissures
3. One for overlooking
4. A furrow between the left
5. A depression for the gall
6. A superficial cavity
7. A great swallow

Q. What is the course of circulation?

A. From limb to limb and back again.

Q. How is the voice performed?

A. The voice results from the vibration the air suffers during its passage when expelled from the lungs. Are you going to ask why the air suffers? Why it was expelled?

R-SPIN: A Collaboration for Music & Dance

(The Revised Speech Perception in Noise Test)

The helplessness is its own kind of dusk There is a slow shadow descent to send And the sounds of the night are full and empty with nightmares of feral dogs and cemeteries He smells like kerosene in my mind The sound of letting go Smell the carousel The kerosene The careening of arms and legs in the back of the car Circled and encircling I think I am drowning

I think I am drowning when they come at me with the headphones And it sounds like I am drowning Everyone's lips are moving Covered I listen to the world that speaks hushed Like listen letting go We are out running a thunderstorm Tell me What do you hear And with what ear do you hear it

This that and other things / such (about the actions of the listener or about ideas expressed or understood by the listener) / like that / that sort of / in that manner in the interior

Give the following commands: Pretend to blow out a candle Pretend to hammer a nail Comb your hair

The doctrine of consent and the doctrine of the common good
This self This body that wants to choose I want to replace my
voice I want to open my mouth and be surprised when language
comes out I went I want you to know that no matter how
incomplete the sentence may feel May sound I have spent my
whole by trying to speak it I am afraid

He told me that doctors have determined that the voice in our
mind is not ours In our mind the voice is not the thing that tells
the body how to act The body has already made its own decision
That sound interprets It interrupts Not cause but reaction We are
always naming ourselves What do I trust now I want to tell you
Here is the bone Here is the cliff The cliff is not a bone

The woman considered the NOTCH

Sue was interested in the BRUISE

How long can you hold your BREATH

Bob was cut by the jacknife's BLADE

The girl should consider the FLAME

He smelled like kerosene His skin tasted like the fire Show me your bruise They are scared of the dark and want to be visible They covered my ears and asked me to listen I didn't want to be bound They are scared of the dark and want to be visible They covered my ears and asked me to listen Why are they asking so many questions My tongue is dry and Why are they asking so many questions My tongue is bitter

Fluorescence Ask me a question It's the taste of flat orange soda Peroxide Hypothesize We build a hunker hunger To pursue with intent of capture I chase that word I chase Tell me It's a hang up Tell me this hung up attempt The friction of a hurdy-gurdy against the hush

He might consider We can't consider She is considering

Tell me everything you see going on in this picture
Tell me what happened to bring you here

Miss Black would consider the WRIST
Ruth hopes he heard about the HIPS
Tom won't consider the SILK
Paul hopes she called about the TANKS
They had a problem with the CLIFF

I went to the garden and waited One small body to see I only
know how to talk to myself And only I know how to talk to me I
will give him the sentence to say And he'll say it back to me And
then we will say it together He considers wait I beg for forever I
say begs He hears thanks I am dictating this back to him

That time of night in the summer when the birds and cicadas
coexist They speak and I cannot speak back Mid day and midnight
might be one in the same I sent my tongue to a boy in a tree once
You might as well keep it The tree I said You wouldn't like what
I say after this anyway I sent my tongue Go with me beyond the
bois Beyond the stumble of an empty utterance The stubble of
my teeth caught tight

Leave me on a short rain Lead me on a short reign The dirt in our mouths makes our thoughts clean Makes our words un gasoline He told me I was buoyant I could be thrown in and rise to the top I wasn't afraid of anything Was that a dream That looked like the ocean or a puddle in the forgotten neighbor's yard You mistake falling down for death You mistake falling down for an early plea an aerie play

Say / Show me your

Shoulder

Cheek

Ear

Nose

Knee

Candle

Bear

Peanut

Shirt

Ant

Tulip

A body forgotten the word Show me your whisper Show me your kneel The amount of information lost I am happy to be sewn I am happy to be shown That I am sewn shut

Linoleum That almost burning smell Afraid of cups coming toward my ears When you muffle the world Your mouth moving without sound I can't listen I am trying to hunt Caustically isometric The line in the mind between the isolate and the irrupt I know I know the word for face Yours Ask me the same

The holder of the savage memory has lost its selvage Semiconductor of a self-willed self-same eruption More this evergreen remission Mortal permission to let go of names Semi-undone Remade and re-educated As a forgetful one I am the sleep deprived toddler fumbling through space

Do you think you can be helped? / This great need for inference / Is this an insect? / Does it keep you warm? / Does it have a window? / Make a fist / Point to the ceiling then to the floor / Put it back

I am going to read you a short story and then I will ask you some questions about it Are you ready?

I catch this goddamn telegram like a bug in my ear Some sort of buzzing from a far off place I put my hands over my ears My ears I stick my fingers deeply into the canal and still And still the buzz buzzing like a fly trapped against the window glass He keeps sending letters to my silence address I address the fire There is the burn of sleep And sleep sleeps like a slow burn of forgetfulness He smells like kerosene in my sleep In my skin when I put my nose up close to my hand I don't have any matches I don't have a way to match the sound with the word with the answer with the idea with the forget with the arm with the eye that looks past the ear Please take them off me I hear too much Who needs my voice when everything is already a forest fire

Repeat after me Your heavy wish I'd tell you that I cannot become I cannot but the death of an idea of a wish I am your misery company Ask me how The witness tree The surveying of our landscape of motion away From the burden of communication

We might be riding together I want to believe in this random act of motion Of the motion of our eyes averting Away from each other No one can look But we all listen We all hear the stick stuck grasp of wheels

Spread some butter on your BREAD
He tossed the man a ROPE
We've spoken about the SCARE
He is thinking about the ROAR
Miss Brown wants to talk about the HINT

What's the point of all this glass if there aren't eyes for it If there aren't ways to trap it To keep it locked in a wind-up box If there aren't I want to keep for myself If I speak You take my words Every single one Every single one of them a tragic figure

It's six o'clock He comes home They go between two others They are where they should be I sense kerosene It looks as if nobody is around What color is it?

Tell me What do you hear And with what ear do you hear it?

Proficiency Badges

Inspired by the *Girl Scout Handbook: Intermediate Program* (1947)

We had cut down a tree. At first, we were building dams. But as suddenly as the tides had risen, the water fled. Had I asked? In those days, you questioned even the ocean. Had I made it up? But it had moved in, and I had bathed you in it, in the basement. Back then we had names that were parts of ourselves. I called you *man of war*. And then, just as suddenly as it had consumed us, youth expired. And then we had to make a fire.

My skin asked questions about the heat. And gave up waiting for the answers as it sloughed off its scales. Skin shows a remarkable willingness to expand as the blister fills—with water. A fire that is water.

We are terrible at endings. And so we imagine them all the time. I convinced myself the woman this morning with the broom was going to step out in front of the train. She kept saying, "It's coming." Like she wanted to reassure us.

Man of war, where are we going? Why do we move corners and wait? My skin carries the names you have called me, every half muttered breath that was a wish. It is the part of me that feels most old. A twitch in the eye that has a memory of that time when we made our life out of fallen branches.

Cherish the strangers. Who stop and motion. The ice too thin. Their gestures that arrive as acorns, a something to bud, to extend, to become sunlight aspiring for the unfurling of a small hope. When the stranger says, *I just had to tell you*, I know that I did something right, that the bottle left the shore and was picked up by a small girl in a canoe on an inland pond. We are both saying—hello out there. Hello.

It is a series of compromises, which is somehow deep affection. That is, I have knit this cloak and you cannot see my eyes. Every time you say you are giving me a gift, I know that you are asking me to give a gift to you. My pleasure is never mine. It is an answer to a call. Do you beck, do you beg? We are weft and then unwound and left, sprawling.

I cannot become anything further but a quiet note. A turntable records us wondering if the needle is bent, pointed, is drawing the lines as it goes.

Even in this sun, I can almost see the snow. The earthquake of the mind and its constant tremors. I am still new to death. Once, I dreamt of the dying days before his death. He wrote and said, "I'm going to read your book. I'm going to ask if I might make time for such a thing." It is probably not the book you would have wanted to read. He said there are names for things. You will know how to call it when it comes.

Brother dust, brother sand, brother skin grit. Shame is our shadow. We make our own mercy.

How to make a body, a boat. The slanted slats of a barrel, burned. What will I carry in my berth? Will we wash ashore to find that we are the hulls of since shucked buildings we once knew?

I remember that day when the world decided it was against itself. And from then, death has for years craved nothing but death. Children made in its image.

I set myself to sun to make a language of curtain movements and slat peering. I know you, fire, old friend. I know you, shiver of fog. From ash we began to fashion the tools of structure. I am hammer to your nail.

Those are poisonous to the touch, but don't confine your interest to the flowering plants, those carried by wind, by water, by insect. Those carried only by my self. Fingertip to fingertip to mouth. The anemone, the windflower. Nature covers a scar made on the face of the earth.

Is it auto for some to be biographical? A good scout goes in search of. Hears that voice in the woods. Goes and finds just the sound. You tell me about the hunt. The prey and parry. Tree trunk to tree trunk to blind. When a scout goes blind in the woods, is there a knot we can make with our tongues to say come find me?

I've managed to make it all about me, the fire, the broken ice, the distant cracking of axe on log. When you sent up a flag, I knew it was right flank, not surrender. We took the whites of our eyes and made them a signal. We blinked a Morse code of stitches. I carried a splint in my pack.

You're afraid of the sounds of the ocean, its radio. I don't mind the fear of nothing, the fear of infinity. Are they the same? The dream sludge of color left behind.

Forget the casualties of the storm. Forget what withers. Did we levee that dust behind? What I ask of kindling, I demand of string. A recipe book for a lost who.

The magnet ocean. It pulls our thoughts undoing. It can never be quiet, humming with voices sending out their frequencies. It's not the silence of sleep but the throws and threads of a million lost conversations.

I am gritting the failures into dusty grains. We will go in boats in the night. I have my trust in a man of war, while my fear is in the woman of actually. Nerves like salt flakes evaporated.

There are many ways to make a sick person comfortable. Try thinking of other ways. You found the hatch in the roof. I hoped the eclipse gave way to absence. That when the clouds moved, there was nothing left but a shovel we had used to bury the fire. Can we decamp? Tearing down the tent is as important as erecting it. How do we pack it all up and leave without the tiniest trace? Ask the trees to tell no one.

Beauty is a split, a tear, a peeling away to an opening, an exposure, a way out or in. A mouth that has given up words in exchange for chewing.

Let me go to sleep. Please, this once, let the winter be the sleep, bleeding into the snow.

What is the sound of flimsy, fluently, rolling, wet? The mouth opening and closing, in sleep and in hunger. The breath of a dancer born out in feet.

When nails and hammer are not at hand, the archer's knot or timber hitch. To tie your own parcels. To put together a broken thing, an animal. A good knot should be tied quickly and untied easily. Take up the slack of rope with your demeanor. Although we have never been able to control the weather, we listen to the radio, the farmer, the traveler, the shipper, the sailor, observe accurately and practice constantly.

There was a war horse we knew how to bridle, to ride. We flanked the forest. Tell me that cannons are but flashlights we match with our fingers. Push here and listen.

I think we'd forgotten how red blood can be. How many shades it takes, how many textures. We ran thick, we ran like knit, like spider webs. We gave it by the bag, by the cloth, by the mouthful. I was dirty. We are more blood than water than salt than breath.

I wish I'd never been young.

Lighting candles in the belly of the whale, respite even when swallowed. Striking bones for flame. The hum of moving through the magnetic waves.

To have given voice to campfire. We were children of flame in and flame out. How much can a group of young girls destroy? And how much can they rebuild and make to grow with hands of seeds and pockets of string?

Tuck me into leaf. What may the fall forget, be forgotten. We were heroic once just for being willing to run. We stormed the fields while they burned.

When the fever comes and our skin is burnt, who will shut my eyes?

You were rolling a cannon. We were digging a trench.

I made a rainy day box. If we found a lost child or had been bitten by a dog, why should we obey? We observe whether there are dangers. We know how to drive a nail. Know the proper care and handling of barn lanterns. Know how to sharpen a whetstone. We are able to name the parts of our animal.

Will we take the side of the children or adults?

An ice lake of a mind. Take a razor's edge across it. Take a pick axe. Build a hut far out on its extremity. Start fishing.

To scout a river, to ford a body between beginning and end. To make myself akin with a whisper. To yawn or shout or gulp or scream. A cry of many volumes.

This is the fear of too much goodness. We are waiting for disaster. We are unknitting our bellies. Unspooling strings of blood. Making a yarn of our curse. We paint the damp night after the fire goes out. We are handprints on trees. We are the markers of stakes in the ground. To hammer and unhammer and bleed and reap and sew and needle. To quilt the bunting of a smock that can't quite fit.

We've come to the hunt. It's your turn to go and hide. Let me not hear you in the brush. Do not be mistaken. I have been given arms, which is to say that I have been given a how-to, an instruction manual for walking deep into the woods, calling out to you again and again as my voice fades to smaller and smaller. And then, run. Be the thing of memory. That phantom we will both debate. You will say you heard me laughing. And I will say that I was shivering in fear.

All paths lead to the body. It is a handbook, which is not to say that it is the only reference, reverent we know. We take instruction lightly. We light pilot lights in other's stoves. I am not a girl you can construct from marginalia or from ghosts that find in your sleep. I burned the books. Tore out their pages and threw them in random dumpsters in the city. Pockets full of lockets emptied one by one. I donated them, gave them up, gave them over. Words can't give a blind man sight.

It's the splinter you can feel but cannot find. This is how girls are made: with axes and kindling. This is how women are made.

You might become knots. I might become sails. This might be but a tiny rowboat on a small lake in the middle of a state that doesn't recognize me. I know how to paddle. How to gig. And how to take the hook from the mouth. How scales stroke bloody the palm of the hand. You sleep in the moss beside the sounds of fish gasping for air.

Will I be let alone in the woods? How do I ask to be forgotten? Underneath this pile of leaves, I've been storing books and handkerchiefs and ziploc bags of dry cereal, life savers. I am squirreling. I want to be what's buried and forgotten and dug up only later when it's old and beyond use. Tear the tether.

I know about your injuries. How many blades, at what speed. At what distance. You tell me how you failed to bandage it with one hand. How much it bled.

I came from the summer of brush fire, raining ash on my forehead. Every day I could have made a cross.

Dear man of war, how do I dictate order by absence?

Hello filament. We've wrapped thread around our fingers. We can touch the hot things, the jagged things, the broken glass that moves between destruction and unravel. Hello flicker. Under box, under bed, under screen. That fly we can hear but cannot find. The wings anxious. Trap, trap, trap against the window. We are waiting again for snow. Blowing on our hands and saying *any minute now*. Any minute now, the fall. The shiver. The crack.

The skin peels back and waits here. We make new wounds. This is a seed. How to make a stitch. To unpry the fingers of a dead hand. When the snow won't come no matter how heavy the clouds. When the winter just sits in the wings. And the birds come by early and never leave. And the garden does not know when or if to give up. I keep asking the frost so that we'll all know and agree, it's over. It's time.

Plan a real or imaginary overnight trip. Pack and stow. Dramatize the courteous and correct. Be able to explain a clear and thrifty message. When stranded in a strange place, know at least three of the whistle signals used on a boat. And how to use waiting rooms. Demonstrate that you know how to say thank you graciously. Know how to know if you are lost. Know the fare, the accommodation.

I am mindful of an oncoming, a very distant or not so distant mechanical movement of steel. Let it be the weight of many tiny things.

Let it be the clog, the jam, the stick stuck in the ticking of history. A spoke in the wheel of a desperate move. To replant the forest. To replenish the night. Do you know how hard it is to hurt no living thing? Every hiker wants her arms free. To carry only what she can put in her pockets. I know it has many uses, a tourniquet. An apron.

Being able to follow a trail is one of the oldest skills in the world.

It was meant to be an adventure. When you think it's madness and it turns out to be church bells. And you ask for the cold to become the bone, the fuse, to make the snow the ligament that stretches our need. We freeze with fire.

The snow has the power to prove how the tiny, piece by piece, can cover you. I say we are ash. And always have been.

Acknowledgements

I would like to extend my deepest thanks to the editors of the journals and outlets where many of these poems first appeared: *American Academy of Poets, Dalhousie Review, Dusie, Five Points,* the Poetry Foundation and the "PoetryNow" podcast, *Thermos, Typo,* and *Under a Warm Green Linden.* Thank you to Meekling Press for the beautiful artist book edition of "Proficiency Badges," and thank you to the International Museum of Surgical Science in Chicago for providing me during my residency with the essentials for a poetry pursuit—a little desk by a window and a library key.

I am also grateful to Heather Lang-Cassera, David Pischke, and the Tolsun Books family for welcoming me in and for their kind and generous attention to my poems.

Carrie Olivia Adams lives in Chicago with her husband and two cats. She is the Promotions and Marketing Communications Director for the University of Chicago Press and the poetry editor for Black Ocean. Her books include *Operating Theater, Forty-One Jane Doe's,* and *Intervening Absence* in addition to the chapbooks *Proficiency Badges, Grapple, Overture in the Key of F,* and *A Useless Window.* When she's not making poems, she's making biscuits.